MW00596419

A
Different Kind
of Same

A
Different Kind
of Same

A Country Girl's View
of the World

KELLIE KUNZLER

BAR JK PUBLISHING

A Different Kind of Same: A Country Girl's View of the World
Copyright © 2023 by Kellie Kunzler
All rights reserved, including the right to reproduce
distribute, or transmit in any form or by any means.

Except as permitted under the U.S. Copyright Act of 1976, no part of this book
may be reproduced, distributed, or transmitted in any form or by any means,
or stored in a database or retrieval system without the written permission of the
authors, except in the case of brief passages embodied in critical reviews and
articles where the title, author and ISBN accompany such review or article.

For information contact:
kelliekunzlerauthor@gmail.com
www.kelliekunzlerauthor.com

Published by:
Bar JK Publishing

Copy Editor: Heather Randall • Content Editor: Debbie Ihler Rasmussen
Cover design by difrats
Interior book design by Francine Platt, Eden Graphics, Inc.

Hardback ISBN 978-1-958626-49-8
Paperback ISBN 978-1-958626-51-1
Ebook ISBN 978-1-958626-50-4
Audio Book ISBN 978-1-958626-52-8

Library of Congress Number: 2023913639

Manufactured in the United States of America

To my family:

*Del, Will, Danie, Nick, Brad, Emily,
Kassie, Cherilyn, and Hope.*

*Thank you for letting me include your
stories as I share mine. I feel blessed
that I get to claim you as mine.*

Dear Reader,

Isn't it funny how life can take a turn that you weren't expecting?

I started sharing uplifting messages on my Facebook page in an effort to help people put aside their differences and focus instead on what we all have in common. Many of you let me know you appreciated my words and the difference they made in your lives. So, I continued to post things occasionally.

And somehow, I ended up here, with a book full of my life's observations!

It's my greatest wish that as you read this book, you will be able to feel God's love for you.

I am grateful for this gift God has given me, and for His promptings to share it with you. This book is my way of helping spread some good in the world. I hope you enjoy it.

Kellie Kunzler

JK

Fitting In

———————

HAVE YOU EVER felt like you didn't fit in?

"I Was Country When Country Wasn't Cool" was a popular song when I was growing up.

That's how I felt. I was a cowgirl that didn't feel like I fit in with the other girls. I lived on a ranch and grew up wearing Wrangler jeans and cowboy boots, and I usually wore a ball cap or cowboy hat because we worked most days out in the sun.

The other kids listened to rock 'n' roll, but I liked country music. I learned how to drive a tractor and a feed truck out in the fields or on dirt roads instead of a car on the town streets.

College was another huge adjustment. Living with all those people on campus was so different for me. I was studying to become a secretary, and I struggled to wear the expected professional attire; I'd much rather wear my jeans and boots.

I spent all my spare time at the college live-stock center, where I was most comfortable. It felt more like home than any other place. On top of everything else, I was the lone country girl in my apartment, making it a challenge to fit in with my roommates.

Church meetings were another place I felt like I stuck out like a sore thumb. I was the only girl that went to church wearing western-style dresses and boots.

Though I felt out of my element much of the time, I did try to find the positive things in those experiences. I considered it a challenge to be true to myself while trying to find a way to get along with others.

My dream had always been to marry a rancher and continue living the lifestyle I loved.

After college, I did just that. We've raised a family and worked hard to keep our fifth-generation ranch going. But like everything else, figuring out how I fit in with my husband's family and the ranching operation was an adjustment.

I really wanted to show I could help, and I was ready and willing to run the swather to cut the hay, but that was my father-in-law's "job!" He was quite territorial. To this day, I've never swathed the hay on our family's ranch. It was passed on from my father-in-law to my husband, sons, and daughter-in-law.

Like most people when they get married and start a new life, it took a while for me to find my niche in the community. I was one of two people who could play the piano well, and that really helped me find a place to fit in. I started teaching piano lessons and loved working with the kids. Singing came easy, so I joined the choir, I became a 4-H leader, and my home-made brownies became a hit at the community potlucks.

Eventually, I found more ways to fit in on the ranch and in the community and made many lifelong friends.

My struggles to fit in throughout my life have made me more aware of those who are "different." The people everyone seems to notice and who are usually the life of the party are easy to see in a crowd.

But I notice the quiet ones who sit in the corner (usually because I'm sitting next to them!). They are the ones who dress differently, the ones who seem to feel uncomfortable and have a hard time joining in.

It took a few years for me to realize that we all struggle with "fitting in."

Every person I have ever met has had to "find their place" in the world. Each stage of our life brings opportunities and challenges to find how to fit in.

Along with everybody else, I still struggle to fit in with some groups.

The most important lesson I've learned so far in my life, especially since 2020, is that while we all have differences, we also have many things in common. One thing, we are all children of God who want to be loved and accepted. We all want to fit in. Once we realize this, it's the beginning of seeing each other in a new way. Being more understanding, patient, and kind to each other is easier.

When that happens, we end up changing the world for the better!

JK

The Long and Winding Road

How did you get to where you are right now?

Looking back at my life's journey, I didn't anticipate some of those twists and turns I had to navigate. I hoped my life would follow a little straighter path. But it didn't. I've seen some beautiful scenery along the way, but I've also been through some pretty dark tunnels and forests where it's hard to see the light.

Sometimes I can see where I want to go, but I still have to follow the winding, slow-moving path because the deep washes, boulders, brush, trees, and other obstacles make it impossible to use a shortcut. It may take me longer, but I'll make it.

I once heard a talk from a guy who worked cattle in southern Utah. He described the rough terrain and how they had to follow the winding trails when moving the cows because there were no safe shortcuts. The destination might only be a quarter of a mile away as the crow flies, but the route took several hours, including challenging turns and switchbacks.

He told of one experience when they took a shortcut, but in the end, they added three more days to their job. (The shortcut caused more work and added more time to their journey.) What appeared to be a good idea wasn't the wisest course after all.

This message had a special meaning for me. I really wish to use a shortcut on my journey. But there are certain things along the winding trail that I can't learn any other way.

For those who love hiking (I respect you all!), the trails aren't usually straight and easy. To get the best scenery views, we must put in the effort and work to reach the destination. It's not easy. But it's worth it.

When faced with trials, we can learn so much; we can't learn any other way. My life has not turned out how I imagined it would. I've had challenges I never thought I'd have to deal with. I ask God, "What is it you want me to learn from this?" (Sometimes, it takes me a while to figure it out. Some things I'm still trying to figure out!)

There is a song by Garth Brooks titled "The Dance." I love this song because I can relate to it so well. I love to dance! But when you realize the dance symbolizes our life, it brings an even deeper meaning. The song's last lines remind us that we could have avoided pain, but we would have had to miss the dance. It's still worth it no matter what we must go through. All those winding roads will eventually lead us to something better.

I've told my family I want this song played at my funeral.

There is a scripture that brings me comfort. In Joshua 1:9 it reads, "Be strong and of a good courage; be not afraid, neither be thou dismayed: for the Lord thy God is with thee whithersoever thou goest."

I'm not alone, and neither are you! No matter how tough the trail gets, Jesus is by our side. And those rough patches are where we'll learn the most and feel the closest to Him.

This journey isn't exactly what I planned for my life, but I wouldn't trade what I've learned for anything. And when I finally reach my destination, I'll know much more than when I started!

Trust in the Lord

THOSE WHO KNOW ME WELL would probably tell you that I tend to be a serious person and that I always have been.

Early on I learned that life is filled with difficult and hard times. Part of this stems from my dad being diagnosed with cancer in his saliva glands when I was around six years old. Dad was thirty-nine.

When Dad was preparing for his first surgery, he asked the doctor, "Since you're operating in that area anyway, would you see what the lump is behind my ear?"

The lump had been there for most of my dad's life, and the doctor agreed to check. What they found was a mass of cancer, and the doctor realized this was where the cancer most likely had originated.

Dad had several surgeries and radiation treatments that affected his vocal cords, leaving him with only the ability to whisper. He loved to sing, so this was extra hard on him.

Due to Dad's treatments, our normal daily routine changed, and my younger sister and I spent a lot of time with my cousins. Mom would drive her morning school bus route from Almo, Idaho, to Malta, then she and Dad would drive to Pocatello for Dad's radiation treatments and be back for her afternoon route. I remember going with them one time and Dad introduced me to the hospital staff. Even as a child, I could tell the staff liked my dad and talked with him and Mom like they were friends.

Now as an adult, I look back at that time in my life and have a new appreciation for what my parents went through during that incredibly difficult time.

The day my dad died will be forever etched in my memory.

Dad had not been feeling well and was in the hospital in Burley, Idaho, forty-five miles away. Mom was there with him. My seventeen-year-old brother had taken the two-ton truck full of harvested grain into town to be processed and was going to check on them. We were hoping the doctors would release Dad.

I was eight years old on Saturday, October 4, 1975, when my two sisters and I were cleaning in hopes that Dad would be coming home soon. Since my grandparents lived twenty-five miles away, we were surprised when they came to the door. It wasn't like they just happened to be in the area. I was excited to see them but couldn't figure out why they were there; however, after a few minutes, they gently told us that Dad had died.

Honestly, I don't remember exactly what was said or at what point I left the house, but I ended up at my favorite spot when I wanted to be alone—the sheds near the corrals. Under one of the sheds was an old flatbed truck.

I climbed up on it, sat on a hay bale, and I started to cry. With tears streaming down my face, I asked God why He took my dad. I told Him we needed our dad pretty bad here with our family.

I don't know how long I talked to God, but it seemed like a long time to me. I finally decided that if Heavenly Father needed him in heaven more than we did here on earth, then He would help our family be okay without our dad. I had to put my trust in Heavenly Father.

About the same time I finished my talk with God, Grandpa and my little sister came to find me. She didn't seem to realize what was happening. I could tell Grandpa didn't know what to say to a little girl, but he tried to comfort me as best he could.

I didn't realize at the time how momentous that decision to trust God would be for me throughout my life. I have relied on Heavenly Father and Jesus to get me through some really tough times. I know I'm not alone because everyone has something big to deal with at some point in their life.

Over the years, I have watched people as they've faced their own hardships and adversity.

Not everyone chooses to turn to God for help getting through those trials. I wish I could share the comfort I feel by seeking His help.

Which type of person are you? Have you chosen to trust God?

The peace that can come through putting our trust in Him is real. The trials may not go away, but when we choose to trust in the Lord, we can receive the strength to keep going. He is aware of each one of us! He knows what we are facing. Trust that things will be okay no matter what happens.

Trust Him!

Why?

ONE OF THE MOST asked questions is "Why?" I remember feeling the weight on my shoulders when my oldest child was born. We named him Will, and I knew I was responsible for caring for and teaching him. As his parent, I would teach him how to walk, talk, ride a horse, and drive a truck. But there was more; I needed to teach him about Jesus, right from wrong, and how to be a good person.

As soon as he learned to talk, Will bombarded me with questions. I noticed that no matter what I asked him to do, he wanted to know "why." I remember being so frustrated with him because he wouldn't do anything until I explained why.

I often used the phrases "because I said so" or "just do it anyway."

I needed him to trust me, and I would explain later.

I catch myself asking "why" when Heavenly Father asks me to do things. I want an explanation first, like Will. (I guess he gets that from me.) Heavenly Father and Jesus ask that I trust them and understand the "why" later.

In September 2019, I felt a prompting to return to school, and I knew it was coming from my Heavenly Father. Of course, I asked "why" and listed all the reasons I couldn't. But patiently, He prompted me again; He even let me know what I was to study. I complained that I had no extra time for school. I was not only caring for my widowed, elderly father-in-law, Dee, but I was scheduled for shoulder surgery.

Finally, I committed to go and prayed He would show me the way. By the end of November, my shoulder was healing well, and Dee had returned to heaven at the age of ninety-four.

God had opened the way.

I enrolled in an online college program in January 2020 and graduated from that course in December of that same year. I continued my online education and graduated with my bachelor of science in professional studies and an associate degree in family history research in April 2023.

I still have no idea why Heavenly Father asked me to return to school. I have met some wonderful people who became dear friends, and I've learned a lot, but I don't know what the result will be. I realize I need to trust Heavenly Father, and He will explain later.

Do you ask "why" when God asks something of you? Maybe to get a new job, move your family, or other significant changes in your life? Has He asked you to forgive someone?

What God asks of us is rarely easy, and it can take a lot of faith to be obedient.

It's okay to ask "why." But sometimes, we need to trust and obey. God always has a plan; we'll understand the "why" later.

JK

Knowing

HAVE YOU EVER had times when you "just know" something? It might not make sense to anybody else, but you "just know" what you're supposed to do, what will happen, or how things will work out. I have come to know that these moments are gifts from God.

The first time my future husband took me home to be with his family for the weekend, I felt this was where I belonged. I "just knew" this was home. Looking back, it's good that I felt that way because it took him over a year to propose finally! (That's another story.) My family and this valley where we live are truly gifts from God.

After I had my fifth child, I "knew" there was still one more child to come to my family. Years went by. I wondered why God wasn't sending us another baby. After ten years and several miscarriages, I got pregnant at age forty-three.

Twenty-five weeks into my pregnancy, the doctors told us something was wrong. They said I could lose the baby at any time for the next eight weeks and that she would be disabled. They even suggested an abortion. I knew my baby was a girl, so I wanted to name her Hope or Faith.

I was on a journey that was testing my faith, but I was hopeful that things would be okay. I "just knew" that in my heart. Hope was born at thirty-three weeks, weighing two pounds and one ounce. She was small but whole and healthy and had to spend six weeks in the NICU. She defied what all the medical people told us to expect. Hope truly is a gift from God.

Everyone at some time, in some way, has received these gifts from God. Do we recognize them for what they are? Are we clinging to that knowledge, even when it doesn't make sense to anyone else? In James 1:17 we read: "Every good gift and every perfect gift is from above, and cometh down from the Father of lights." God wants to help us. He is willing to guide us. Are we willing to listen and accept that guidance?

Over the years, I've learned a lot—some of it the hard way. But I can honestly say that in those times that I've "known" certain things, I've held tight to that gift when it didn't make sense to anyone else but me.

How grateful I am for those gifts from God that let me know in my heart the paths I was to take.

JK

Get Thee Wisdom

I GREW UP on a ranch and worked cattle on horseback, but I'm not an expert rider or trainer.

Once while watching my kids participate in a horse event, one of my sons came over by me and observed for a few minutes. He then commented that one of the horses needed a different bit, and it would quit fighting its rider. He then pointed out how his younger sister needed a bigger saddle. Once he pointed out these things, it was easy for me to see how making these two changes would improve the performance of the horses and the riders.

After my first child was born, I became an emergency medical technician (EMT). My husband, and now my sons, help man the rural fire department. Our crew has helped fight many fires over the years. There have been times so many of us wondered why the guys in charge didn't send their crews to certain spots and get on it fast enough. Their decisions just didn't make sense to us.

But then the EMTs were required to take fire training to man the ambulance on a fire. After I watched the training videos, it made perfect sense why those in charge made certain decisions. They have learned through the experience of fighting fires and have seen enough tragedies that they know what they should or shouldn't do.

So many of us see what we want to see, or we get focused on what makes sense to our limited knowledge. When we do this, we miss out on opportunities to expand our understanding. Are you convinced your view and expertise are the complete picture?

I've been watching a popular TV series, *The Chosen*. It's about the life of Jesus and His disciples. It is very well-written, and for me, it has

taken these people we read about in the scriptures and made them real. As Jesus gathered his
disciples, some accepted His teachings while
others were perplexed about Him. Interestingly,
one of the Pharisees, Shmuel, is convinced that
he's saving people from being deceived by Jesus,
whom he accuses of false prophecy. He makes
it his mission to expose Jesus as a charlatan. I
think it's safe to say that Shmuel didn't know as
much as he thought he did. Even the disciples
Jesus called to follow Him, who believed He
was "the One," did not fully understand what
that meant. Each disciple assumed Jesus would
do things a certain way based on their beliefs
and knowledge. It soon became clear that Jesus
wasn't exactly like they thought He would be.
But they were willing to learn from Him. This
is probably the most essential part! Their will-
ingness to follow and learn from Jesus is what
sets them apart.

I know I'm capable of learning more! In
Proverbs 4:7 we read, "Wisdom is the princi-
pal thing; therefore, get wisdom: and with all
thy getting get understanding." This scripture

reminds me that it's not enough to learn something; we need to understand what we are truly learning. For instance, I can read Spanish quite well, but I don't know what all the words mean. I just know how to pronounce them correctly. We can apply this to our scriptures too. We can quote scriptures, but we are missing the point if we don't truly understand what they mean. I hope we will be filled with the desire to keep learning.

After all, we don't know what we don't know.

Advice

WHAT'S THE BEST ADVICE you've ever received? I've had a lot of wisdom shared with me over the years. I even found a magnet that reads:

"Good judgment comes from experience . . . and a lot of that comes from bad judgment."

– COWBOY WISDOM

How true!

A friend told me once that the best advice she had ever gotten was from me. I remember thinking, *Really?* Then she shared what I had told her, and it went something like this, "When you get upset at someone and want to chew them out, wait a couple of days. You can always chew them out later if you still want to."

I don't remember where I heard that, but I've tried incorporating it into my life. Sad to say that I even needed to, but it has made a difference for me and sounds like it has for my friend.

Growing up, when someone would be mean to me, I wanted to chew them out, but my mom would always tell me not to retaliate and to just let it go. So, I did. When I got older and felt safe to voice my opinion, I did that too—more than I should have. Somewhere along the line, I realized that maybe that wasn't always the best idea.

We should all realize that our words and actions have consequences. Stop and think about what you want to accomplish. Do we have to tell someone what we don't like about them at that moment? Or ever? Emotions run high, and things are often said in hurtful ways. But if we hold our tongues and ponder what happened, we can usually see things in a different light. Having another perspective and taking the time to choose our words carefully can benefit everyone. And praying for help will give you the added guidance you need.

I have had several conversations that could be considered confrontations. Some didn't go so well. Others left me feeling peaceful, even if the other person was still upset. The difference in this was that I took a few days and sought divine help beforehand, asking for understanding to know what to say to improve the situation. I entered the conversations more open to what the problem was.

One incident that stands out in my memory was with my mother-in-law. I lived next door to her and knew I wanted to have a good relationship with her. And for the most part, we did. But there were moments!

One involved a situation when I took a stand, and my mother-in-law was unwilling to admit her part. We needed to talk, and I knew it could end badly, so I prayed for guidance and help in what to say. Did it go perfectly? No. My mother-in-law's pride wouldn't let her admit she might be wrong, but I left the conversation knowing I had done everything possible to make peace. And oddly enough, by the next day my mother-in-law and I were on good terms again.

How many of us stop to think before we act or react? Is that moment of lashing out in anger or hurt worth it? Are we okay with burning those bridges? Is that really what we want? Whatever we do, we must accept the responsibility and consequences of our actions.

Now, my kids might read this and wonder who this person is that's sharing such great advice. Their mom is known to get after them at times. But I really hope they can see how hard I'm trying to be better and do better. I know they think I'm getting softer because they think their little sister, Hope, gets away with more than they ever did. (I'm neither confirming nor denying!) I like to think I've gained some wisdom at this point in my life. After all, I've made my share of imperfect judgments, and through each experience I've gotten a little closer to understanding how to use good or better judgment. I appreciate all the great examples I have had in my life to learn from.

Thank you all for your patience!

Walk a Mile
in Someone Else's Shoes

WE OFTEN HEAR the phrase "Walk a mile in someone else's shoes to understand them." This has always made sense to me. No one really understands what another person is going through unless they have experienced the same thing or at least something similar.

As children, we learn not to touch a hot stove through actual experience or learning from someone else's. When I see someone get hurt, I immediately start thinking of when I have had something similar happen and remember how it affected me.

My six weeks of experience with my preemie daughter, Hope, in the NICU has given me the capacity to have greater compassion for those parents going through the same thing. Our experiences are different, but it's safe to say we probably had the same feelings worrying about our babies.

Many times, we didn't know how the bills would get paid. There just wasn't enough money. This can be a private thing for some people. But if you've ever been in that position, know you are not alone. There are a lot of people who do understand what you're feeling.

When I see someone being bullied, it brings back memories of my childhood. (When I was a kid, we said we were "picked on.") I was that child, and I remember how I felt. I want so bad to take away their pain. If there are times I can intervene, I do. I may not be able to stop it for them, but I can make sure they know, at least from me, that someone does care about them.

Trials give us experience, and there is something to learn from each one. We can empathize with and teach others going through similar trials.

I have appreciated the advice I've received from people who have hit the same rough spots, potholes, and barriers as me. It is important to help others. God wants us to share the lessons we've learned. And the best advice is when it's given with love.

All my life, I've had issues with my feet. From the time I was a little girl, I always wear out my right shoe first. Because of that, I can only wear certain types of shoes. At the age of thirty-nine, my right ankle shifted, and I was walking on the side of my foot. My mobility was limited and painful. I found an ankle specialist at the University of Utah who recognized my condition and got me an official diagnosis. He fused my ankle and changed my life. But my right foot is still much smaller than my left. So, technically, I can't walk in another's exact pair of shoes, and they wouldn't be able to walk in mine either—but I appreciate it when people try to understand me and what I'm going through.

When we look for the similarities of our experiences and don't pass judgment because of our limited understanding, we are one step closer to walking a mile in their shoes and loving thy neighbor as thyself (see Matthew 22:39).

JK

Does It Really Matter?

━━━━━━━━━━━━

*H*AVE YOU EVER worked on a project with someone and realized you each have a different way of accomplishing the same goal?

When my husband and I were first married, we quickly learned that we didn't always think or do things the same way. The first time we bought a furniture kit, I realized I needed to be quiet and hand him the tools. Trying to help with my advice was not contributing to our relationship. By the second and third furniture/bookshelf kits, we decided that I would just do them myself. It was less stressful that way, and both my husband and I were much happier.

Did that mean my way was right? Not necessarily. My husband could put the furniture together, but how his mind processes information differs from mine.

It's easy to get upset because someone doesn't do something as we think they should. Does it matter? If the job got done, isn't that the goal?

Growing up, I spent many hours in our farm shop and the fields, helping my brother repair equipment. I was the hold-this, hand-me-this, and go-get-this gopher. By age fifteen, I could order exactly what parts we needed and catch it if they tried to give my mom and me the wrong part. It was a fifty-mile trip to the parts store, so we needed to take the right one home.

One summer day, I was swathing by myself, and a section broke on the swather knife. I knew I couldn't keep cutting hay until I fixed it. I had helped my brother fix one many times, so I rode the motorcycle to the shop to get the parts and then returned to the field. I was pretty proud of myself when I fixed it and could finish swathing the field.

Later, when my brother got home, and I told him how I'd fixed the knife by myself. Instead of being impressed, he let me know I should have done it differently. I remember thinking, *But I fixed it! Can't you be grateful and tell me I did a good job?*

When I got married, I was introduced to the Dee and Del way of fixing things. Del is my husband, and Dee is his dad. I had to adjust to their way of doing things on the ranch. Let's just say it was slightly different than I would have done, but I still got the job done.

One time when Hope wanted to make cookies, I was in class and couldn't help her. I encouraged her to do it alone. When I returned to the kitchen to see how she was doing, the cookies were mixed, but I noticed the eggshells were almost intact. There was a tiny hole in one end of each shell—she had forced the egg through the hole instead of cracking them on the side of the bowl. She got the job done her way.

Many of us are so focused on how we would do something, which is always the best way, that we forget there might be another direction. It's our attitude to those differences that we need to work on. What if the other person did figure out a better way? Are we so caught up in being right that we can't see how anything else will work or how our opinion affects others? Does it really matter?

Does God expect all of us to do things the same way? No. Our diversity enriches all our lives. Remember, Jesus did things differently than the people were used to or what they expected from the Messiah. But we can all be united in following Jesus. We can live His teachings and follow His example. If we do that, it's guaranteed we're doing it right!

Change

THERE IS A SAYING that the only thing constant in life is change.

Once I'm comfortable with a situation, I don't like change. But, to grow and become who we are meant to be, we must accept it.

When I was about forty-three, I strongly felt things were about to change. Our five kids were in school, I was staying busy, and I thought I had a little breathing room and free time. It was also a difficult time financially.

This feeling was so powerful that I worried it meant we would lose the ranch and have to start over somewhere else.

Then I realized I was pregnant, and it all made sense. No, we didn't lose the ranch, but my life changed. Our youngest daughter, Hope, is a blessing. I'm very grateful, but my life is different now than I thought it would be all those years ago.

It was just a few short years later that our life changed again. My hardworking husband, Del, came in after evening chores one day and told me his arm was going numb and there were moments he couldn't make it work right. He figured it was a pinched nerve and decided he might see a doctor the next day. I knew right then something was really wrong because he never wanted to go to a doctor.

The hospital was one hundred miles away. My oldest son and I finally convinced him to go to the hospital that night instead of waiting. When we arrived, he was taken to Salt Lake City by helicopter. He'd had a stroke.

Though Del recovered quite well and can work on the ranch, things are different. Our family has had to make some adjustments. Del was fifty-six years old when he had his stroke. Will was twenty-one; Nick, eighteen; Brad, sixteen; Kassie, fifteen; Cherilyn, twelve; and Hope, two.

Will cared for the ranch, his elderly grandpa, and his younger siblings, who also pitched in to help out, while I stayed with Del in the rehab center for ten days.

After months of therapy, Del regained use of his right hand and taught himself to write again. He still can't saddle his horse, but with his sons' help he can still ride and move the cows. For years Del put up most of the hay by himself; now he helps with some of the swathing and hauling, but he doesn't have the strength and stamina he used to have.

The plan was always for our sons to run the ranch, but they were given the opportunity at an earlier age than we expected.

We're not perfect at it, but we're trying.

Sometimes change is forced upon us, and other times we choose to make the change. Either way, it provides an opportunity for us to become better people. I have grown in these last few years, but it hasn't been easy. Growth requires effort and struggle.

Heavenly Father encourages us to do the same, just like we encourage our children to learn and grow with change. He wants us to become more than we are. More kind, more thoughtful, more caring, more loving, more courageous, and more faithful. His goal is for us to become more like Him, and this doesn't happen if we dig in our heels and say, "No thanks. I'm fine right here."

Change can be scary and hard. But, if we trust God to lead us through it, we will be blessed.

Change changes us.

Flaws and All

SOCIAL MEDIA wasn't around when I was growing up. Those years were hard enough for me without worrying about what people worldwide thought about me. Today I read things other people share about their lives, and I can't help but wonder if there is more to their story. Some only share how wonderful life is; they think people won't like them if others know their reality. Some want to escape into a fantasy life created online for various reasons.

One of my struggles was carrying a child to full term. I have six kids, but I've had more miscarriages than live births. It wasn't until I was bucked off the horse and didn't ride for a while that I finally got pregnant with Will, my first child.

Eventually, I realized I had to stay off the horses and bouncy tractors to carry a baby. I was willing to do this to have a family, but it was hard to watch other women riding horses at eight months pregnant or other things I didn't dare do. At the same time, it hurt that one of my neighbors would have a child the same age as the one I lost. I've struggled with envy and asked God, "Why me?"

Then when I did become a mother, I didn't always act the way I should. I'll never forget the day I was upset at four-year-old Will, grabbed his arm to make him do what I'd told him to do, and accidentally pulled him into the doorframe, giving him a fat lip.

That brought me up short, and I was mortified by what I'd done to my son! I remember telling him how sorry I was, and his reply was, "It's okay, Mom, I forgive you. I know you didn't mean to hurt me."

I shed more tears than he did that day. It took me a while before I dared share this experience with anyone because I was worried others would judge me as not a nice person. If I had shared that on social media, I would have been charged with child abuse. This experience helped me see what changes I needed to make in my life. Today, I know I'm a better version of myself.

Some things are personal, and it's okay for us not to share them with everyone. But we can all try to share our genuine selves in hopes of connecting with other people.

Remember, there is someone who knows exactly who we are. God sees the real you and loves you, flaws and all.

Give Grace

WHEN YOU LOOK BACK at your life, do you see moments that really made a difference for you? I have several.

Some of the ones I'm most grateful for were when I deserved to be set straight on how I was acting and when someone chose to be patient with me. We all regret how we've acted, but if we can learn from those moments, they can become blessings in disguise.

When I was first married, I wanted to fit in with everybody else in the valley. I was excited to be asked to help prepare a meal for the ladies' church group using my grandma's recipe. I remember wanting everything to be just right and give the impression that I knew what I was doing. I also remember when things didn't work out quite right, I let my frustrations get the best of me.

To this day, I will be forever grateful to one lady who helped me in the kitchen. She calmly made simple adjustments ensuring the success of the meal. She didn't scold me; instead, her presence helped calm me.

I'm also grateful for my sisters-in-law, Cheryl and Marilyn, and their unending patience with me. I'm much younger than they are and made my share of mistakes at family gatherings. They never criticized me or the way I raised my children. Thankfully, my older kids survived to tell the tale, but I'm not finished yet; I still have Hope to raise.

I will never forget the kindness of an elderly lady in our valley. We were at a community dinner, and I was talking with one of my family members. I excitedly told them how the elderly lady had met her husband; I thought her love story was so sweet.

I was still learning everyone's stories and didn't realize how wrong I was with that one!

She overheard me, and she motioned me over to sit by her when the dinner was over. She kindly told me the full story of how she and her husband had met.

Then she said, "I didn't want to correct you while you were visiting, so I wouldn't embarrass you, but I wanted you to know the true story." It has stuck with me for over thirty years.

Oh, how grateful I am for the grace these women showed me. You probably have someone in your life who has shown you grace, and I'm sure you have also shown grace.

I hope so.

But there is One who has promised all of us the blessing of His Grace. "For by grace are ye saved through faith; and that not of yourselves: it is the gift of God" (Ephesians 2:8).

Jesus shows by His example how to treat people, and He loves us all. I hope we all get a chance to make this kind of difference in someone else's life.

Assumptions

ⓞNE SATURDAY MORNING, I attended extrication training with the Utah Fire and Rescue
Academy. I wore turnout gear and learned to
break windows and cut doors off vehicles.

Since I became an EMT, I have participated
in this training several times through the years.
It was a good refresher course, even if I mainly
just observed. It was fun watching two of our
sons, Will and Brad, learn how to use the equipment and safely tear apart a vehicle to access a
patient in an emergency.

Later that day when I asked Will what he
thought about the class, he said he liked it, especially learning how to use the equipment. My
first thought was, *What do you mean? You've*

helped on the emergency crash truck before. Then I realized that even though my boys helped on the fire and crash trucks, they had yet to use some of the specific equipment. That was the first time they and several others had ever used those tools. They received valuable training and had fun doing it.

I had assumed that since I knew about extrication, my sons did too. I had forgotten that they had never received the official training. I realized I had expected them to already know what took me years to learn.

We often do that—assume others know certain things because we do. That isn't fair, because we all learn at our own pace.

Years ago, when my older kids were teenagers, they participated in a celebration with the youth performing several dance numbers. They had to put time and effort into learning the dance routines and rehearsing on the football field with a few hundred kids. With that many dancers, you can imagine how rehearsals went.

A couple of weeks before the performance, they held a dress rehearsal. I arrived early to pick up my kids so I could watch the practice. It was neat to see that many people doing the same movements to the music. Then I started to notice something. As hard as they tried, only some were on the same beat or moving together.

The choreography was the same for all of them, but some dancers were behind a count or two.

But guess what? They all completed the moves and finished the dance. They might not have been in sync, but they all arrived at the same place.

I thought about how we are all on this earth, trying our best to do good things and get back to heaven. We are at different points on our journey, but we are headed in the same direction. And even though we might still be learning the dance moves, we may not all be on the same beat. Doing the steps will eventually bring us to the dance's end.

God does not expect us to know all things right now. He has a plan, and He sent Jesus to teach and lead by example. "But the word of the Lord was unto them precept upon precept,

precept upon precept; line upon line, line upon line; here a little, and there a little" (Isaiah 28:13).

Like a child learns things a little at a time, so do we.

It makes sense that I would have more knowledge than Hope, my youngest child. It also makes sense that my testimony of Jesus Christ would be stronger than hers. Hopefully, I can share my knowledge a little at a time to help increase her testimony of Jesus.

Hopefully, we all share our testimonies of Jesus Christ, our Savior, with someone. Please don't assume they already know what you do.

Christmas

I LOVE CHRISTMAS! I love the lights, decorations, songs, and Christmas trees. My uncle Thern cut fresh Christmas trees every year, and we always got ours from him.

When we visited Santa just before Christmas, I remember trying to figure out how he always seemed to know so much about my family and me. Every year he pulled through with the presents that we asked for. It was magical.

Through the years, I've met several people who declare they don't like Christmas. They feel that the focus is not on Jesus and that it is too commercialized, and they won't even put up a decoration. I understand how it can be very overwhelming if we let it be.

But I don't agree with those who think we should eliminate Santa Claus. To me, Santa embodies all the things my Heavenly Father is. Santa loves children and wants to give them gifts that bring joy and gladness to them and the world. If you think about it, Santa bringing gifts symbolizes Heavenly Father giving us the gift of His Son, Jesus Christ. And what we receive from Jesus is His atoning sacrifice, forgiveness, and eternal life.

My favorite Christmas show of all time is *A Charlie Brown Christmas*. As a kid, I was so impressed that Linus could recite the story of Jesus's birth that I also wanted to memorize that passage. It is in the Bible in Luke 2. Our family reads this passage every Christmas Eve; then we watch a fun Christmas movie while we get ready for Santa to come.

Another favorite Christmas memory is from when I was a teenager. Each year, my mom would make some goodies and put together baskets for the older people in our valley. That year, I was the one chosen to deliver them.

Christmas music was playing on the radio, and the moon shone brightly. I had just given Ivan and Barbara Darrington a gift and visited with them for a while.

I was in the car heading home when the song "O Holy Night" came on the radio, and as I listened, the Spirit touched my heart. I knew then, and I know now, that Jesus was born. He lived, and He gave His life so that we, too, might live again.

So, when I hear Christmas music or see Christmas decorations, I automatically think of the birth of Jesus, the Savior of all mankind. The Spirit of Christmas, to me, is the love of God. It is the Spirit of Peace and Good Will to All Men.

This is the Spirit I wish we could keep in our hearts all year long.

JK

Discouraged

IF YOU ARE DISCOURAGED, let me suggest you watch the movie *Secretariat*.

A few years ago, I struggled with something I was trying to accomplish. As we watched that movie about a racehorse, I found myself relating to one of the characters, Penny Chenery Tweedy.

She was doing her best to be a good wife, mother, and daughter. Her father was sick, her mother died, and her life changed. She stepped in to run her father's struggling horse farm. Many people tried to tell her she should sell and that there was no way she could make it work.

Then, when her father died, those closest to her—the ones she should be able to count on for help—became her biggest antagonists. Everywhere she turned, they told her to quit. But she believed in her horse and herself and was determined to figure out a way to make things work.

She didn't quit!

We watch *Secretariat* every few months, and each time, the message impacts me just as much as it did the first time. Don't give up! I've learned this lesson repeatedly and should have it figured out by now. But each time I'm faced with a new path or goal, I still struggle to find the confidence to make it happen.

In my first year of college, my English professor gave me negative critique on my writing. It has affected me all these years. I was so discouraged; I was scared to write anything.

Shortly after I was married, I was stuck waiting in the truck while Del checked on the cows. I decided to write a poem about an experience we had with calving. It involved a freezing night and three very cold calves. We warmed two of them in my kitchen and one in the bathtub.

I wanted to prove to myself that I could tell a story and write poetry. My husband liked it, and so did my family. Ideas came to me, and I wrote a few more poems. As I found the courage to share them with more people, I continued to receive positive feedback. Since then, neighbors and friends have asked me to write a poem or a history of different events. I'm grateful for the encouraging comments, especially from those who read my social media posts. I guess what I'm trying to say is that if you want to do something, go for it. Don't let other people discourage you.

Secretariat was the Triple Crown Winner in 1973. It had been twenty-five years since one horse had won all three races: The Kentucky Derby, The Preakness, and The Belmont Stakes. As of 2023, Secretariat still holds the record in all three races. We wouldn't have Secretariat's inspiring story if Penny had given up on that dream.

I think it's a safe bet that we've all met resistance and obstacles while trying to accomplish our goals. But, if one door closes, check for an open window. And if you don't know where to go next, pray for help. God is ready to help us.

When you feel discouraged, remember that quitters never get to be Triple Crown Winners!

What Is Your Why?

I SHARED A MESSAGE with a group of women at the Utah Farm Bureau Women's Conference. After much prayer, I knew I needed to ask them these questions; we should all consider them.

Now, these questions can apply to anyone, but since I'm a rancher, I continued my message with something I'm involved with—agriculture. I hope you can see how they apply in your life.

The main question is: What is your why?

What is it that keeps you working and trying, never giving up?

When things get complicated—and they will—why do you not quit?

Why is it worth it to choose your lifestyle?

We can list all the pros and cons of why we are involved in agriculture, and the list of cons will probably outweigh the pros. But to me, the pros are more valuable. They might be fewer, but they truly outweigh the problems.

There are so many life lessons that we learn by taking care of the land and our livestock. We know about life and death, the value of hard work, and what can happen if we are not diligent in doing our jobs. We learn responsibility. We know the joy of doing a job well and seeing the harvest. We feel joy at watching a new life begin.

We learn teamwork because—let's face it—we can't do everything by ourselves. We need help. After doing everything we know how to do, things can still go wrong, and we can lose our crop, someone can get hurt, and our livelihood threatened.

During the calving season, we see the loss of many calves, causing our hearts to hurt for the loss of life. We often wonder how we can keep going. That is where faith and hope come in. Usually, people in agriculture tend to have a close relationship with God. We rely on our faith, hoping for a better year and harvest. We recognize there is a higher power who watches over us.

Stop and think of a time when something could have been disastrous, but no one got hurt, or things looked bad but still worked out.

I recall the times my kids or husband have had close calls on a four-wheeler or horse and should have been badly hurt but came away almost unscathed.

I recall when Del and I had been at a meeting in town, and I got a phone call from my second oldest child, Nick, who was in his teens. He told me he'd had a wreck with the "red" horse. I asked if he was okay, and he said he was, just a little sore. I wondered which horse he meant by the red one.

Then he explained it had wheels, and I realized he meant the four-wheeler. Nick usually liked to be on his horse, but that day he had decided to take the machine to get a cow in quickly.

He got too close to the cow, which kicked the four-wheeler as he was making a turn, causing the four-wheeler to turn over on its side. I was glad he was okay, but then I thought, *Really? Dad and I leave the ranch together for one day, and look what happens!*

I believe these are our miracles from God. He does not take away all our troubles, but He will help us through whatever challenges we face.

As I've pondered my why, I thought of a poem I wrote fifteen years ago. I want to share some of it with you; maybe some of you feel the same way.

"My Life"

All I ever wanted was to be a rancher's wife,
And raise up a family in the cowboy way of life.
To be able to work side by side with the man
Who gave me his love and took me by the hand,

To teach our children how to respect and love the land,
And see the beauty in the creations of God's hands.
To honor our heritage and carry on the traditions,
And pass this legacy on to the next generation.

I want each of my children to know what it feels like
To sit their horse and see the view from the mountain height.
To look out on a field of newly swathed hay,
And feel the freshness of the earth right after it's rained.

To watch the baby calves frolic in the snow,
And harvest in the grain that they helped to grow.
To go to bed 'bone-tired' from working hard all day,
And feel the satisfaction of paying their own way.

I want to give my children a sure foundation,
So they can stand strong when faced with temptations,
And be known as men and women of integrity,
Who lend a helping hand when someone's in need,

To know where they're going and why they are here,
And find the courage to face their fears.
I want to see them happy, doing what they love,
And raising their families with help from above.

I want to go to sleep at the end of each day
Knowing I tried my best to live the right way.
I want to make a difference somehow, someway,
In someone else's life that I've met along the way.

And when I leave this earth, when my time is done,
And I'm back in the presence of my Father and The Son,
I want to say the words, and know that they are true,
I finished everything I came here to do.

— Kellie Kunzler, 2008

To me, there is no better way to teach values to the next generation than to raise them on a farm or ranch. In the process, we are also feeding the world. What a great combination!

So, when you think about your why, make sure to remind yourself that you don't have to be perfect. Just do your best, and God will help with the rest!

Communicating

M FAVORITE MOVIE of all time is *The Man from Snowy River*. Who hasn't dreamed of capturing a wild horse and "breaking him in." Of course, falling in love with a cowboy was nice too.

In the movie, they used the term *horseman* to describe the best rider—someone who doesn't just ride a horse but who understands it and works with the animal in harmony. Clear communication is key to this relationship.

I have been part of a conversation that lacked clear communication. (Actually, there have been several.) My youngest daughter, Hope, was telling her sister and me about a character on a TV show, and we kept trying to correct her. We knew she was wrong, and we were right.

After going back and forth for several minutes, she finally said a phrase which made it clear to us what she really meant. And guess what? She was right, and so were we! If she had just communicated those exact words to us initially, we wouldn't have reacted the way we did.

I told Hope had she said those words in the first place, we would have known what she meant.

She said, "I thought you already knew."

We often assume someone understands what we mean, and we also think we know what others mean. Misunderstandings happen every day, usually because we are quick to jump to conclusions. If we are really listening to what someone is saying, we are taking the time to understand what they are trying to tell us.

There are many ways we communicate. We use our words, tone of voice, eyes, facial expressions, and body language. We're all familiar with the phrase "Actions speak louder than words."

What are your actions saying?

Picture a rider pulling back on the reins of a horse while at the same time kicking him. That poor horse isn't going to know what he's supposed to do.

But when the rider gives clear directions, communicating exactly what he wants the horse to do, they work in harmony. Watching a horse and rider who are in sync is a beautiful thing. I think Heavenly Father keeps hoping His children will figure out how to communicate and work in harmony.

When we finally do, it will be a beautiful thing.

JK

Connections

---

*A*RE YOU COMFORTABLE meeting new people, or are you convinced you will have nothing in common?

At a conference I attended recently, we were to find someone we didn't know and find five things we had in common. My first reaction was to hide in the corner because I didn't think I would have much in common with anyone.

But I'm getting better at talking with strangers.

An older woman sitting at the next table asked to be my partner, and we began visiting. We learned that we both play the piano and the organ. We share an interest in genealogy and have several children—her, seven; me, six—and we raised our families on a ranch. We live in the same county, and she resides in the same area as my cousin and knows her well. Wow!

I also reconnected with someone I'd met at the last conference six months earlier. She had been my partner there, and we realized we also had many things in common. She is very special to me, and I was so excited to see her! Best of all, I could see how much happier she is now than she was then! She has dealt with many difficult situations and is able to smile as she continues to move forward. I've learned so many things from her. As we parted ways this time, we promised to stay in touch.

Every time I pair up with someone new, I make a connection, and my life is enriched. I'm not sure why I am still initially uncomfortable letting people get to know me. I have no problem asking them about themselves, but I'm always worried they will judge me and find me lacking.

But when I focus on finding common ground, I always find something. I now love making connections.

I'm thrilled when I can help others by connecting with friends. I have a niece who was getting ready to run a half-marathon, and she mentioned she wished she knew someone she could ask for advice.

I don't run at all, but I have a dear friend who is a master at it. So, I was able to connect the two of them. Even though my running friend was struggling with serious health issues, she gladly talked to my niece, who I know will benefit from the advice. The connection helped them both for different reasons.

The funny thing is, I was nervous to get to know my running friend because I thought she wouldn't be interested in getting to know me. After all, we were too different. But the joke was on me. She is an inspiration, and I am so grateful for her friendship.

No one is exactly like anyone else. Our life's journey is our own. But, in my good and bad experiences, I have learned things that make it easier to understand others. Each new friend I make along the way enriches my life in more ways than I can count. The trick is to figure out what we have in common.

If we remember that we are all children of God, it should be enough to start the conversation and make a connection.

COWBOY LOGIC:

Not all cows have horns, but it doesn't really matter. Horns or no horns, they are still cows.

Storms

ONE MORNING as I drove my school bus route, I watched as storm clouds moved in along the mountains from the northwest corner of our valley. It brought back memories of watching the storms roll into the Almo Valley, where I grew up.

Being in agriculture, storms that bring moisture are welcome sights unless we're harvesting. The one that morning didn't amount to much, but it got me thinking.

There are different ways to know a storm is coming. We can watch the clouds move in, and the wind blows the trees. Sometimes we can smell it in the air. Other times, we can feel it coming because of the ache in our muscles and bones. But occasionally, a storm comes in so fast that we get no warning, catching us off guard.

We all must weather the storms of life. No one is spared; some deal with health, some with finances, and others with relationship storms. Some are mild, while others can get severe. Sometimes we have time to prepare, and sometimes we don't.

What storms have you dealt with? A diagnosis of cancer or some other disease? Loss of your job? Infertility? Loss of your home? Abandoned by your friends? Cheated on by your spouse? Loss of a loved one? Do you feel like God has forgotten you? These are just a few that we may encounter throughout life.

Some storm clouds can undoubtedly turn into tornados or hurricanes. Remember, though, that people do survive even the worst storms.

One of my favorite lines comes from The Nitty Gritty Dirt Band's song "Stand a Little Rain." It tells us that to see a rainbow, we first must endure the rain. Fun fact: The Nitty Gritty Dirt Band once played a concert where only seven people showed up. I was one of those people.

Sometimes we forget that rainbows only come after the storm—and that storms are an essential part of life. And we must remember that they are only a small part. Rainbows are too.

No matter the storm, there is light beyond the clouds. In John 8:12 we read, "Then spake Jesus again unto them, saying, I am the light of the world: he that followeth me shall not walk in darkness, but shall have the light of life."

The light of Jesus Christ brings hope, relief, and joy. And the best part is that He wants this for all of us. So, when you feel like the storm you are in will never let up, remember that just beyond those clouds is a light ready to provide you with a rainbow. We are never truly alone, even when it feels like it.

But we see a rainbow only after we've weathered the storm. What a beautiful view to look forward to.

In Tune

*H*AVE YOU EVER heard a piano that is out of tune? I have an ear for music, and when an instrument isn't tuned properly, it is hard for me to enjoy it. A guitar is easy to tune, but a piano needs a skilled tuner.

One thing every musical instrument has in common—they need regular tuning. None of them can stay in key forever if only tuned just once.

Can a person come to know God through just one prayer? Some may say yes from their own experiences. Others might say no; maybe they didn't receive an immediate answer or the one they hoped for.

Typically, praying just once will only give us some of the answers we seek or provide the foundation for a firm testimony of Jesus Christ. Communicating with God through prayer can bring untold knowledge, peace, and blessings.

Reading the full set of scriptures available to us today was quite an accomplishment for me. I was relieved the day I finished reading the Bible because so many parts were hard to understand. I remember thinking how glad I was that I was done and could move on now. Ha! I was much younger than I am now. Little did I know that was only the beginning of my learning.

Thankfully, I've been drawn to read the scriptures many more times since. I especially love to reread parts of the Bible, like the New Testament and the words and teachings of Christ. Esther's story is also special to me, along with several verses in Proverbs. Each time I go back and reread these words, I gain a new understanding.

I've heard it said that if you want to talk to God, then pray, and when you want God to speak to you, open your scriptures. I know this to be true. How sad would it be if we only opened them once?

Just like any musical instrument, our spiritual life needs regular tuning. Each season of our lives brings new challenges and questions that we need help with. When we pray or read our scriptures, we can gain a new perspective, giving us more guidance.

And for those times when you are struggling so much that all you hear is an off-key version of your life, remember that it is normal to need a good tuning now and then.

You may be like the guitar, easily tuned, or maybe you are like the piano that needs someone else to help you get in tune.

Either way, the results will be "music to your ears." After all, it's easier to hear God when we are in tune.

A Light in the Dark

I LOVE SUNSETS! That moment when the color of the sky starts to change from just barely blue to gold, pink, red, or orange. God wanted all His children, no matter where they lived, to experience something beautiful every day.

It is a gentle reminder that God is watching over and loving me.

I also love the moon and stars. I'm blessed to live in the country and have a field behind my house. I have an unhindered view of the Big Dipper, Little Dipper, and the North Star from my backstep. I don't know all the names of the constellations, but I love looking at the stars. And I think the Milky Way is amazing. When the moon rises and works its way across the sky,

I'm so grateful for the light it gives, dispelling the darkness.

You see, I'm afraid of the dark. Technically, I'm scared of what can happen in the dark, not the darkness itself.

But no matter how small, any amount of light gives me hope that things will be okay.

When I was growing up, my family had a band and played for dances. We would travel anywhere from five to two hundred miles away to entertain. Of course, usually, we would drive back home in the dark. I remember laying my head against the car door and watching the night sky as the miles passed.

I was always comforted when I could see the stars and the moon. I would thank Heavenly Father for giving me a night light, and I wouldn't be so scared.

As I've grown older, I'm still fascinated by the night sky. I still look to the heavens for comfort and hope. And those nights when I can't see the moon and the stars shining through the darkness, I cling to the expectation that the light will come in the morning.

I believe the light represents God's love for all of us—that we are God's children and carry some of that light within us. When we meet someone struggling, we can share the radiance within us. When we do, we can remind them of who they are and how much they are loved.

We are all on this journey called life together. No matter how hard we try, we can't do it alone. I'm so grateful for those who shared their light with me. I'm especially indebted to those willing to walk with me through the darkness. But most of all, I'm thankful for those who have used their light to strengthen my own when it threatens to go out, fueling mine till it shines brightly again.

It's my hope that I can bless others by sharing my light with them.

Acknowledgements

THIS BOOK was just a distant dream that has finally became a reality with the help of many people.

Thank you to my family for keeping things going while I shut myself up in the office writing. They are my inspiration, and I love them very much!

I want to thank Richard Paul Evans for creating a group to help writers become published authors. He is a force for good, and one of the nicest people I've ever met.

Thank you to Debbie Rasmussen for her friendship, for answering all my questions, and for teaching me what it takes to become a published author.

I also want to thank all my family, friends and neighbors who liked what I wrote and encouraged me to keep writing. You are too numerous to list here, but your names are written in my heart.

And finally, I want to thank God for guiding me on this journey. Anything I've gotten right is because of Him.

About the Author

KELLIE KUNZLER was raised on a ranch in the little town of Almo in Southern Idaho. She grew up helping on the ranch and singing in her family's country western dance band. Her love of reading started at a young age and opened up a whole new world to her beyond the mountain valley where she lived.

After graduating from college to be a secretary, she met and married her cowboy, Del Dee. Kellie and Del have six children, and continue the tradition of raising cattle and horses in Rosette, on their fifth-generation ranch in Northern Utah.

Kellie recently earned a bachelor's degree while studying family history research. She plays the organ and piano for her church congregation, is an AEMT on the ambulance service, and is a 4-H leader. She also drives a school bus for the local school in Park Valley. Kellie spends most of her time writing, helping out on the ranch, and being a wife and mother.

JK

Printed in the USA
CPSIA information can be obtained
at www.ICGtesting.com
LVHW091812301023
762155LV00001B/1